# Coal Town
# Photograph

POEMS

## Pauletta Hansel

DOS MADRES

2019

## DOS MADRES PRESS INC.
P.O.Box 294, Loveland, Ohio 45140
www.dosmadres.com    editor@dosmadres.com

Dos Madres is dedicated to the belief that the small press is essential to the vitality of contemporary literature as a carrier of the new voice, as well as the older, sometimes forgotten voices of the past. And in an ever more virtual world, to the creation of fine books pleasing to the eye and hand.

Dos Madres is named in honor of Vera Murphy and Libbie Hughes, the "Dos Madres" whose contributions have made this press possible.

Dos Madres Press, Inc. is an Ohio Not For Profit Corporation and a 501 (c) (3) qualified public charity. Contributions are tax deductible.

Executive Editor: Robert J. Murphy

Illustration & Book Design: Elizabeth H. Murphy
www.illusionstudios.net

Typeset in Adobe Garamond Pro & Carpenter ICG
ISBN 978-1-948017-39-8
Library of Congress Control Number: 2019932019

For small town girls,
whether you stay or go.

# Table of Contents

## I.

## II.

# III.

# IV.

# I

# The River

On one side of the road there was the mountain, sliced open and hollowed in places to make room for more road, and on the other side, the river, though nobody called it that. Behind the Dairy Bar, the turnaround spot for the older kids' nightly cruising, it was a sewer. In the spring when the rains brought down runoff from the mines, it was a flood, claiming from our neighbors' basements the things they'd put away for later—picture albums, worn quilts and Mamaw's Singer sewing machine. Afterwards, pieces of cars, mildewed sheets and pampers all found their way to the banks, or to the peeled branches of sycamores hanging above. Leaving the Dairy Bar, the not-river wandered through town, splitting it into unequal halves. That summer I turned thirteen, I pedaled my bike across a rusted bridge to a part of town I'd never heard of, where I saw no one; a wild-west ghost of a town like on TV, with an abandoned train station that was mostly splintered platform and tumble-down bricks, weeds growing up through broken-out storefronts and caved-in houses like turtle shells I'd see smashed on the road. I craved the old town's emptiness and how the pounding of my heart echoed beneath the cicada's shrill song. From there, I'd bike the road along the banks, stopping on the graveled berm with its Queen Ann's Lace and honeysuckle, the flowers of places unclaimed, breathing in my own aloneness. Never had I strayed so far; I thought I'd left it all—my mother's hovering love, the too-muchness of my body. I'd return home dry inside—that solitary self—glistening with my own salt.

# Where Do You Want to Spend Eternity?

All I could imagine was an afterlife
spent in a cedar chest, only the fraying
lace of linen to amuse the hands. Death
is not sleep, they told me. There must
be endless spools of everlasting thought
filling and spilling out into the earth
below, the earth above—no rest
for the dead's restless mind.

Later the cumulus streets of heaven
had not much more appeal,
with gates that opened and closed
like the pearly clasp of Mother's purse,
letting you in, not out,
wearing the clothes they chose
for burying you, with only choir robes
to change into should you burst a seam.

Hell hardly mattered.
I had seen beneath the cast iron
floor of Granny's cookstove,
knew there'd never be eternal life
among those burning coals.

If they had asked before they
lay me down to sleep,
I would have said,
      I'll take my heaven here—
      cool cotton sheets, with quilts
      tucked round and books,
      the ones I never mind
      to read again.

# An Ode to
## Library Basements

and to the girl
who skittered down the steps
those bottomless
Sunday afternoons to lose herself
in possibility.
You made me.
Those windowless
hours spent wandering
the moors, Parisian streets,
the gravity of stars—
the endless alphabet
of other people's lives.
My mother's Sunday roast,
TV's pallid drone
forgotten.
I breathed you in.
      You breathed me out again
            no less
    myself.
More.

# Give It Voice

My first poems
were love poems, too,
but they weren't so much
birds singing
as butterflies—the trifling white ones
out before the flowers
in the early days of spring,
mutely lighting on blades of grass
and the clumps of violets
that spring up everywhere
you look, if you are looking
and the girl I was
was always looking, always
sounding the depths
of her own longing
for Love—with a capital L—
and it took a long line of words—pages
and pages and decades
of words—while meanwhile
up above on the banks
those fluttering wings…
I didn't stop.
I am glad now
I didn't stop
looking or sounding
or writing these poems
even before I learned
to let them sing.

# Villanelle in a Minor Key

My father's favorite songs were in a minor key—
Shady Grove pining by the midnight door,
feet bare on the splintered floor.

At night I'd see my father's cigarette
smoldering to ash beside his stacks of books,
the stereo humming the monks' low chant in a minor key.

He'd been a child no one thought to love.
His people felt it plenty just to take him in,
toughen him up for the coalmine's splintered floor.

Still, my parents packed us up with gifts and lunch
to wind the hairpin curves, the same day back again.
Beneath his breath my father sang in a minor key,

Shady Grove's stockings wound round blue-veined arms,
thin as his mother's that had cradled her boy
before she was laid on the coffin's splintered floor.

My father lived for books and music, and for us.
He never saw the point in the family tree.
My father's favorite songs were in a minor key;
his past was a splintered floor.

# Visit to Cutshin Creek, 1968

Sleeping in is what we town kids do
on summer mornings: sleep until the wash
is done and toast crumbs brushed away,
and mothers take the curlers from their hair
to chat across their fences for awhile
in cotton dresses nipped in at their waists,
fathers forgotten till their tables must be set.
Sleep in, then stumble out to where the sidewalks
blind us as we ride our bikes through town
and to the cool again of friendly houses.

And so sleeping in is what I do on Cutshin Creek,
 this place they've brought me to, with no
sidewalks or fences, where the reluctant
sun remains behind the hills long after morning crows.
Sleep as Granny plaits her slumbered hair
again and coils it like the snake my cousin
pulled me back from just in time, he said.
Sleep while the graveled voices of the men
pull from the house in pickup trucks. Sleep in
till granny's biscuits are cold and the grass
that welts my calves is almost dry and cousins
clamor at my door, amazed she's let me lie there.
Sleeping in's the only thing the same
as town here in the country where my mother lived,
then left, but leaves me to, come summer.

On Cutshin, even words I've learned to count on
come out wrong: my vowels too short, my consonants
too hard to pass here without notice. No matter how
I try to skirt around the men, their laughter spits
at Larnie's girl, plump as their hens and just about as lazy.
My cousins will not give me up so easily. Their voices
try to skip me safe across the slick green stones
of Cutshin Creek and up the steep bank
to the woods my mother loved. They holler down
from rocks and trees she scratched her name in.
But I live too far from this place; farther
than the sixty miles from Cutshin
to the house with shelves of books I read in soft
clipped yards on summer afternoons. And so

I sleep and then pretend to sleep some more
waiting for my parents' car to take me home.

# The Town

I have been gone so long I think perhaps I have invented it, this town, but for snapshots with glimpses of place that frame the people who are the camera's intent. Three nuns in full habit, only the hint of forehead beneath the starched white band. Behind them steps and the wall of a church, or a school. A sidewalk where Easter patent leathers dance. A doorway where I stand, my hair in its passage from white blond to nearly black. All the rest is memory—the wall's red brick; the steep pitch of the roof above the doorway's arch; the ledge I have jumped down from, the one I walk from home to church and back again, to have my picture taken in my new cloth coat and buckle shoes.

When we return, years later—my mother, my new husband and I—the town seems oddly rendered, as if captured in a snow-swirled globe, though it is spring, the redbud barely faded, the yellow green of lawns too harsh against a sky the color of that Easter coat. Yet here it is, the place itself: the church, the school, and schoolyard too—the swings, the monkey bars, the merry-go-round, last year's grass grown up through its splintery slats and at the center where the metal pole has rusted. Forty years ago I lay there, looking up at that same swirling sky.

Even the house we lived in, though twice we miss it, with its added wing, as my husband drives up Main Street and back again, until my mother spots the doorway, just as the photograph remembered.

# Two Photographs

Was I ever that young? And aren't I
now, the way a flower, late fall,
still holds the seed? That girl,
big hair, big glasses, big life rising

from the girl squeezed into the margins
of the other picture, my mother
in the shadow of the kitchen's stone chimney,
everybody's mouth closed tight.

My mother made me that dress I wear in the one,
and her mother made the one she wears in the other,
and on and on behind us. Though it stops
with me.

# Before the River, the Creek

Summer that year
smelled like mayonnaise
down at the end of the holler
where the waters tumbled
through coal-flecked rocks.
I was ten; the world now
a stranger—my body's secret
blood, tang of a screen door
after rain.

# II

# Sister

The heart of childhood beat
not in my own flat chest
but in hers, blossoming
high above
stylishly thin everything else.
Oh, how I loved her! More
even than the Barbies
she said only babies
still played with.

# A Little French

For months I had tried
to find the right mouth,
really any mouth
between the ages of older enough
than me—almost thirteen—
and old enough to be…(my
mind would not allow "father"
to occupy the same space as desire)…
and afterwards
everyone would know
there was something new about me—
*je ne sais quoi,*
a little French, like the kiss
I could not quite imagine,
though I had read the book
my father (that word again!)
left propped against my bedroom door,
*Now That You're a Woman,*
but I wasn't,
not until I found a mouth.
He was eighteen,
home from boot camp,
piled like me into Jane Ethel's latest boyfriend's van
to see James Taylor, live, and all the way,
15, to Mountain Parkway, 64,
a straight shot into Lexington,
between swigs of Boone's Farm Apple,
his mouth was mine.
The rest remained our own—

he had not planned for hands
run through the wig
that hid his regulation burr
and whatever else was in that book
was not enough
to keep me with him in the van
while James sang sweet
in Rupp Arena.
Really, *je ne savais pas*
I was supposed to stay to finish
what was for me,
then,
*accomplie.*

# At Thirteen

I decided to go barefoot,
the way another girl
that summer, '72, might tuck
a flower in her hair
or her bra away inside a drawer.
I can't remember now enough
about the self that chose that path:
maybe barefoot was a fashion
I could hide beneath
the fraying bottoms of my jeans,
or only that there were so few for me
to choose from—my hair too frizzy
to grow long and toss back
from my eyes, my legs
in mini skirt more cherub than Cher.

Even then my body urged
toward metaphor—
I longed to toughen up,
control the tears that roiled
at everything and nothing, fogging
my new glasses. Perhaps the burning
pavement underneath my soles
was salve against a deeper heat.

There was no place to go.
One street through town and back—
daily I walked it,
never looking up to see what they

might think of my bare feet,
the farmers and the miners
come to town, the pool hall cowboys
lounging taut against the doorways
as I passed, eyes down to guide
my feet around their pop tops
and tobacco wads, their stubs flipped
burning to the sidewalk,
their gaze
that rose to linger on the body
in which I could no longer hide.

# Passage

I was fourteen;
they were older.
I was trying hard
to fill the woman's body
I occupied—its breasts
and monthly bleeding—the way
later I'd fill rented rooms
with thrift store furniture.
Nothing ever matched.
Mostly I learned the female art
of silence. To hold my tongue
against my teeth,
my questions veiled
by downturned eyes.
It was easier to pass
for grown with men.
Women wanted to spread
wings to take me under
or to nudge me
from their perches—
no room for three.
Men wanted only
hands against the parts
of me that grew up first.
They were older.
I was fourteen.

# The Honey of Trapped Bees
## (Self-Portrait at 15)

Mostly it's about the bones—ribcage, clavicle, the small knobs on the outside of my knees, a red thrift store pinafore I wear as a tunic, ribbons tied tight at two rungs of bare spine. Mostly, it is tied up tight—my frizzy hair in a bandana, knot of hunger beneath thin layer of skin I pinch and measure, counting its depth. And it is all about what counts—inches and calories; the men, back seats and borrowed beds, and how much more of me they want than I ever want of myself.

# Love Poem (of Sorts) with Cigarettes and Hawk

I inhaled you that winter,
cigarettes I'd pull from your
front pocket, threadbare
excuse for my hand
to your heart, your hand
cupping flame. Near dusk
I walked the hill away,
the chill air burning
in my lungs, to stand beneath
the fire-streaked sky
and let tears come.
Above, the grey hawk circled
close enough for sight.
If he had caught
his prey, you loved me.
Talons empty,
loved me not.

# From These Poems

my body is missing
the gray pain in the night gut
the creak
at its hinges
and all around
those bony places
how it softens
expands even as
a dry creekbed
runs through

# That Winter, Fifteen

I ate mostly oranges.
First my teeth
would tear
through rind—pith,

bitter chalk
on tongue—careful
not to break too soon
the inside. Fingers

peeled away
the rest. I'd pull
apart the segments,
each to be its own

small meal, then bite
through fragile
membrane; pulp
and juice released.

> By spring my flesh
> lay light
> against my
> bones.

That was the winter
I let him tear me open.
I would have told you then
the choice was mine.

# Lady's Choice, He Said

easy or hard, either way
he would take me, so I who'd
already took from his cheap
pink wine, took in his pink cock
too. I knew I was easy.
I knew I'd said no. I can't
tell one without the other.

# Small Town Girl Rap

She's from the backside of nowhere
Not like you'll ever go there
Mountains on the both sides
Town down where the rocks slide
    What's a girl to do
    but get up outta here?

She's from a town with one stop light
Not a thing to do at night
But cruise around the dairy bar
In somebody else's car
    What's a girl to do
    but head up toward the city lights?

She's from a place you don't go back to
Not unless you have to
Move into your old room
Mom says Dad will pass soon
    What's a girl to do
    but what she's gotta do?

# III

# Coal Town Photograph

I am from a place divided
from itself, back stoop
from storefront window
lit to hide the shadow
of the mountain. I am from
the crack in the framed picture.
Which side
are you on—the gone
or the left behind? I am from
a place that could not hold me,
never even tried. Come morning,
mist of evening rain,
a ghost above a mirrored sun.

# The City

After the rain, the alley smelled of wet screen door,
the city-stink of piled up garbage and exhaust
washed nearly clean. She noticed this only in spring.
By summer, the rain when it came
bucketing down made thick mud of the foulness.
The city dug in its heels, spread its muck like
her memory of a garden's red clay.
Next year at this time we'll be long gone,
her father would always say. She'd watch his words
dry out and harden, crumble to dust, and away.
Does he remember last year and the years before,
the same parched yearning? Yet her mother only
nodded. Next year we'll be home for sure,
she'd answer, patting his oil-lined hands.

# When You Ask Me to Tell You About My Father

What's left is the myth of him, the words we use, scrawled symbols
to remind us he was there. A jumble of body parts: skinny legs, a lap,
eyes that were not his without the glasses that left permanent dents
on his Christmas bulb nose, and if he was the heart of us, he turned
into a broken heart too full for its cage. A broken everything—left
shoulder, right hip that would not stop him walking. He had a high
threshold for pain, though his mind was drowning in it, a river pouring
through the doors, and anybody close would have to get a little wet.
Did I forget to tell you about his mother who died of the consumption,
his father who'd come around to drink the money from his piggybank?
Myth, more myth, but that doesn't mean it wasn't true. Did we talk
about his books, or just the Lexipro, before then the *I'm OK, You're OK*
that saved his life back in the 70s? I know we talked about the churches
that he left, though it was never about leaving God, who'd spoken just
to him, told him to read. Books again, more books; so many books we
carted out the door, boxes of them in the weeks before and after. Did I
tell you there was one that slid off his lap when he died? That has to be
a symbol of something, that book, the way it kept getting lost and being
found. Afterwards my mother saved it, labeled with a note she'd written
on a sticky from a memo pad printed with the words, "Things To Do,"
but we found it in her basement, clearing out her stuff, in a pile left
for the trash. *Mind: An Essay on Human Feeling, the abridged edition.*
He'd got it secondhand, his name scrawled beneath the price tag on
the flyleaf, and as it says there in the foreword, "any abridgement
has its unhappy compromises" and this story I'm telling you, it is
not my father, it's only what is left.

31

# Becoming

I first knew I was becoming
my mother when my pee

smelled like hers, undertone of animal
musk. Her perfume, White Shoulders,

scented the dresses she made me.
They swung loose against the body

I swore I'd never need to harness
into shape with elastic and straps

like her. Here we are. Her wisp of body
bound into a wheelchair. Always the faint

whiff of pee. She is letting loose
the weight of flesh. My body

plumps and swells into the mother-
body she is leaving behind.

# Lost

in the thicket
of my body, the girl
I was, unchanged.
How will she ever know me?

# Broken

The morning broken
through lace, sloughed
cells of skin into dust

motes, breaking the light. Life
into stanzas and lines. The book's
broken spine.

The sandstone wall against
the mountain—cracked,
but holding. My father,

my mother broken
from their bodies, from me.
The heart is not complete

until it's broken, somebody said,
a poet or a Facebook meme—
who knows anymore? Years ago,

at 44, I had to find someone
to break my heart again
to let it heal whole.

That year the only gift
that someone gave me—his hand,
molded clay

dug from his land—
broke,
ring finger from palm.

I took it as a sign,
but clung tight anyway,
until the story

shattered. Me with it,
for a while.
A splinter of a dream

dissolved into the wave
and particle of light. The melody
broken from its verse,

still sings.

# Late Marriage

When did I start to snore
and how can you possibly
think it's cute?
You still adore
my breasts when at last
I set them free
to lie loose
flesh to flesh, as we do.

# Motherhood

Fuck,
spit from my own tongue,
tastes milder
than the fucks hawked careless
and unaimed toward my or anybody's face
from someone else's back stoop
(the way my mother years and years ago
flung burning oil that hit the neighbor girl
who should not have been there).
Though I note my stepchildren's flinches
at my forever unexpected gobs
spewed not (as yet) at them—a bloodied
toenail, the kale gone liquid
in the bottom of the crisper, my favorite
series preempted by football
or Trump.
Betrayed, I think,
the way this yellow cat
draped across the lap he thinks he owns
would be to know
that not near so many years ago
the cat I threw across the room
(he had peed in my bed)
did not land on his feet.
Across those years
these children not yet mine
had surely shuddered in their sleep.

# The Single Girl's Bed

Years pass, but in my dreams
the kitchen door still leads
to my first garden, pale zinnias
swoon in the shade; daylilies
ramble through ivy.
My glorious ignorance!
Each year to start again.

# Self-Portrait as a Cockscomb

When touched
seeds spills on the page.
The habitual curve
toward the sun.
Red, of course—
      a bandana
      left in a south-facing window,
      blood just before it dries—
its green days long gone
(no one grows cockscomb
for its green).
This one is plucked from my garden;
my mother's grew tall as children,
blooms as wide as your hand.
It's hard to find those now.

# IV

# The Road

Where I'm from, everybody had a flower garden,
and I'm not talking about landscaping—
those variegated grasses poking up between
the yellow daylilies that bloom more than once.
Even the rusted-out trailer down in the green bottoms
had snowball bushes that outlived the floods.
Even the bootlegger's wife grew roses up the porch pillar
still flecked with a little paint, and in the spring
her purple irises rickracked the rutted gravel drive.
Even the grannies changed out of their housedresses
to thin the sprouts of zinnias so come summer
they'd bloom into muumuus of scarlet and coral
down by the road.

Now driving that road that used to take me home,
I think how maybe it's still true.
Everybody says down here it's nothing
but burnt-out shake and bakes and skinny girls
looking for a vein, but everywhere I look
there's mallows and glads, begonias in rubber tire
planters painted to match, cannies red
as the powder my mother would pat high
on her cheekbones when she wanted to be noticed
for more than her cobblers and beans.
Everywhere there's some sort of beautiful
somebody worked hard at, no matter
how many times they were told
nobody from here even tries.

43

# When She Was Done

there'd be one long bright coil
shiny red as the blood she'd never prick
free with her paring knife, and then quick sliver
moons of Winesap in the fall, anytime else
whatever she'd choose from the produce bin
for what it was not— too soft or too sweet.
And never a cutting board.
One hand for the apple, the knife
in the other, angled away from her palm, slicing
the firm flesh we'd eat before it was mottled beige.

I never learned her trick. I never needed to try.
Grown, I'd bite through the crisp peel with no particular
style all the way to the galaxy of seeds at the core.
Only later—too late—by my own kitchen sink,
I make a mess of it;
my dull knife carves clumsy through skin
her remaining incisors can't break. At the nursing home,
after lunch of gray mush, I slip fat chunks
into the mouth of my fruit-hungry mother,
first biting away the red.

# My Left Hand

Flex wide—
a bird's claw,
tendons beneath the splayed skin.
Less romantic than wings.
Five fingers,
mismatched cousins,
just a little family resemblance
in the chubby knuckles.
A fireplug of a thumb,
circling hungry around them all.
Turn now
the palm with its paths,
its valley and mounds,
low hanging branches
where birds perch
to watch what clings.
Make a fist
to beat back time.
A wedding band
burrowed in a notch
above the joining.

# Remember
## (Rock, Scissors, Paper)

My parents' wedding rings
on my dresser in the jeweled box

where my mother kept his,
until she forgot,

and on the top shelf of my closet
her old sewing shears,

one tip broken.
In her purse I found

a sticky note
printed with the word

    *Remember*

above somebody's phone number,
nobody knows whose.

# Elegy

All things break
away—
Paper loosens
from its spiral bindings,
the music box's key
has overwound, even the good
fountain pen lets loose black
rivers. Cells divide
and spread inside our
secret caves. Parents
die. Children scatter
continents beyond.
Some days there are miracles:
missives, remission, pictures
lost then found
under our Christmas trees;
tea tins, coasters, a father's army tags
retrieved from that vast *somewhere*
our once-precious objects reside.
But mostly not.
Mostly it is up to us to speak
of absent things, to bring
to our neglected pages
the smell of lavender
remembered
in the pillow
where my mother's head
once lay.

# Outside Her Door

She doesn't know how
to be a dog, my stepdaughter tells us

of her own wild child, bristled fur
behind chewed window blinds,

and I think, but do not say,
I don't know how

to be your mother. I try
to remember me at twenty-six, impossible

to be both woman and daughter, blind
battering of walls, searching for the limits

of my own parents' love.
There is so much I do not know,

or say, now that I am nobody's daughter.
I have forgotten all the wrongs

I never forgave them. Blind, still,
to the wounds I surely have afflicted,

mother only to another mother's child.

# The Truth Is

you were easier to love
lost than losing,
easier to hold
when my hands finally set aside
the useless mending of your frayed threads.
The truth is
by the time you had forgotten
everything but gospel songs
sung by the girl you'd been before me,
there was no need
for anyone's forgiveness
anymore.
*What wondrous love is this!*
Sing on.

# Clothespins

Now there's only clothespins to remember us,
dew hanging where the soft parts of our lives should be.

The last one left this morning on the northbound bus.
Now there's only clothespins to remember us

and on the porch, the wringer washer rimmed with rust.
Once our whole life spread across the yard, the world to see.

Now there's only clothespins to remember us,
dew hanging where the soft parts of our lives should be.

# Coal

By the time I knew that coal
was something more than grit and fire
in the belly of the house
and had been held in deeper
vessels than the bucket

that once sent me sprawling
down the cellar steps
and on then to the gleaming room
where the doctor stitched
a crescent moon above my eye;

by the time that coal
was more than just the crack
in daddy's windshield, black rocks
flung from trucks careening daily
up and down our narrow road,

the coal that lined the bellies of the mountains
where our houses perched precarious
as hawks' nests or nestled in the hollowed
places at the joining of those hills
was spent.

Only the ashy seams stitched just below
the sassafras and pine, beneath
the redbud, dogwood, hickory and ferns,
under the leaf-mulched soil and sandstone
still endured.

Now that's gone too,
blasted and stripped away,
the hills a moonscape up above
the sagging houses and the towns.
The road, its hairpin

turns and crumbling berms
is gone as well;
a new highway rumbles through
the place that doctor sewed my eye:
all scars remain.

# The Claiming

On my way out of town,
my car idling at the curb,
I stand where I have stood before,
beside the empty yard.

My car waiting by the worn curb,
I look across the rise and fall of road
beyond the yard, emptied
of my family's home.

Across the rise and fall of road I look
to the cut hill above the town,
my family's last home,
and something in me settles.

The cut hill, the town,
my own, although I never claimed it,
and something in me settles
like dust into the place where what was held is gone,

my own, unclaimed.
Now everything and everyone who bound me here
is dust: the place where I was held is gone;
the girl I was, though I called myself a woman.

Everything and everyone unbound.
I once believed, almost, the lives I lived in houses left behind
(the I who was the girl who called herself a woman)
were still there waiting for me to return.

I believed, almost, the lives in houses (left behind
whenever I had wanted)
waited, still, for my return—
those rooms, the self they'd held—

and whenever I wanted
(although I had never wanted)
those rooms, the self they held
would still be mine.

Although I never wanted
that girl, her body that my own refuses to remember,
she once was mine.
The air that wrapped itself around

the girl-body that my own refuses to remember
(her memory lodged only in mind),
this air whipping round
is all that's left

to carry memory. Mine.
And I can believe, almost, a time
when none is left
to know I've ever been here.

I can believe, almost, it's time,
on my way out of town
with nothing to show we've ever been
here, where I have stood before.

# About the Author

PAULETTA HANSEL is author of six previous poetry collections, most recently *Palindrome* (Dos Madres Press), winner of the 2017 Weatherford Award for best Appalachian poetry book. She was Cincinnati's first Poet Laureate, 2016 -2018 and Ohio Poetry Day Association's 2002 Ohio Poet of the Year. Pauletta is a board member of Dos Madres Press, a volunteer for the Urban Appalachian Community Coalition, with a particular focus on its new Urban Appalachian Leadership Project for youth and young adults, and is managing editor of *Pine Mountain Sand & Gravel*, the literary publication of Southern Appalachian Writers Cooperative. She leads writing workshops and retreats in the Greater Cincinnati area and beyond, including at Thomas More University and as core faculty for The Makery, Hindman Settlement School's new online studio for writers of place. Visit her website at https://paulettahansel.wordpress.com/.

# *Acknowledgements*

Cover Photograph: Anna Harris-Parker
Author Photograph: Josh Miller, courtesy of IDEAS xLab

*Riparian* (Dos Madres Press, 2019): "The River."

*The Lives We Live in Houses* (Wind Publications, 2011): "Where Do You Want to Spend Eternity?"; "Visit to Cutshin Creek, 1968"; "The Town"; "At Thirteen"; "That Winter, Fifteen"; and "Coal."

*Words: Thomas More College Literary Journal* (2016): "Give It Voice."

*Still: The Journal* (2019): "Villanelle in a Minor Key."

*What I Did There* (Dos Madres Press, 2011): "The Town."

*Words: Thomas More College Literary Journal* (2018): "Sister."

*Words: Thomas More University Literary Journal* (2019): "A Little French."

*Lexpomo.com* (The website of Lexington Kentucky Poetry Month, a 30-day poetry daily challenge each June): "Two Photographs"; "Sister"; "Before the River, the Creek"; "Late Marriage"; "Motherhood"; "The Single Girl's Bed"; "Self-Portrait as a Cockscomb"; and "Outside Her Door." "Self-Portrait as a Cockscomb" was also chosen for the print 2018 Lexington Poetry Month Anthology (May 2019).

*Appalachian Journal: A Regional Studies Review* (Volume 37, Numbers 3-4, Spring/Summer 2010): "At Thirteen" and "Coal."

*Boomtown: Queens MFA Tenth Anniversary Celebratory Anthology Queens MFA Tenth Anniversary Celebratory Anthology*: "At Thirteen."

*Undocumented: Great Lakes poets laureate on social justice* (Michigan State University Press, 2019): "Passage."

*Southern Women's Review* (Volume 4, Issue 4: January 2011): "That Winter, Fifteen."

*Literary Accents* (Accents Publishing, 2019): "Lady's Choice, He Said."

*Kentucky Arts Council Where I'm From Project Page*: "Small Town Girl Rap."

*Appalachian Heritage* (Winter 2018): "Coal Town Photograph"; "The City"; and "When You Ask Me to Tell You About My Father."

*The Main Street Rag* (2019): "Broken."

*Words: Thomas More College Literary Journal* (2017): "My Left Hand."

*Poetry South* (2018): "Elegy."

Beyond the usual beloved village it takes to make my poems (inhabited by my fellow writers in my classes and workshops, at the Southern Appalachian Writers Cooperative and Thomas More University Creative Writing Vision Program gatherings and Hindman Settlement School's Appalachian Writers' Workshop, and through the online lexpomo community, among others), there are these influences in particular:

- ~ "Give It Voice" was written in response to Billy Merill's "Give it Wings."
- ~ The first line of "Sister" is from a poem from Ellen Austin-Li.
- ~ "Passage" was written in response to a line in "Bike Ride with Older Boys" by Laura Kasischke.

- "The Honey of Trapped Bees (Self-Portrait at 15)" was inspired by the essay, "All or Nothing, Self-Portrait at Twenty-Seven" by Jill Talbot.
- "Coal Town Photograph" was written in response to Anna Harris-Parker's photograph as part of a workshop led by Rebecca Gayle Howell.
- "Elegy" begins with a line from an essay by Pam Korte, and was inspired by the many stories told one afternoon in my Practice of Personal Writing class (including Mary Hennigan's concept of *somewhere* and all it contains.)
- And, of course, "Coal Town Photograph," "Small Town Girl Rap" and "The Road" draw on George Ella Lyon's iconic poem and prompt, "Where I'm From."